THE CAMBRIDGE MISCELLANY

XVIII

OLIVER CROMWELL

T0349726

OLIVER CROMWELL

AND THE ENGLISH PEOPLE

By

ERNEST BARKER

CAMBRIDGE

AT THE UNIVERSITY PRESS

1937

CAMBRIDGE UNIVERSITY PRESS
Cambridge, New York, Melbourne, Madrid, Cape Town,
Singapore, São Paulo, Delhi, Tokyo, Mexico City

Cambridge University Press
The Edinburgh Building, Cambridge CB2 8RU, UK

Published in the United States of America by Cambridge University Press, New York

www.cambridge.org
Information on this title: www.cambridge.org/9781107660717

First published 1937
First paperback edition 2011

A catalogue record for this publication is available from the British Library

ISBN 978-1-107-66071-7 Paperback

It is no hyperbole to say that the progress of the world towards self-government would have been arrested but for the strength afforded by the religious motive in the seventeenth century.

LORD ACTON, *Inaugural Lecture*

PREFACE

The origin of this lecture was an invitation addressed to me, last summer, by Bürgermeister A.D. Dr Burchard-Motz, President of the Friedrich Sthamer-Gesellschaft in Hamburg, to deliver an address before his society, a branch of the Deutsch-Englische Gesellschaft in Berlin. I gladly accepted his invitation; and I gladly accepted the subject which he suggested to me for the address. The lecture is printed here as it was delivered, on the evening of 17 December 1936. It was a singularly happy occasion. My audience sat at tables, dotted about the room, smoking and drinking beer (it was 'a social evening'); and I lectured all the more happily because I felt that my hearers were comfortable. The lecture was delivered in two parts (the lecturer retiring for rest and refreshment to one of the tables during a brief interval); and I fear that it lasted for nearly an hour and a half. Perhaps only a German audience could have been so generous and so patient; and I owe a very deep debt of gratitude to all who listened to me for the honour of their attention.

The Epilogue was written after I returned, in the four days before Christmas; and the notes were added at the same time. It was natural, after visiting Germany, and talking with German friends for the greater part of three days, to enter into some comparisons which had suggested themselves or been suggested to me. I hope I have written nothing which can hurt or give offence. I had to set down what I honestly believed. A writer can do nothing else...if he writes at all. Perhaps there was no necessity to write. I can only plead that the comparison between the German Führer and our English Protector is one which has been pressed on my attention not only in Germany, but also in England.

I had a special reason for being glad, and indeed proud, to lecture before the Friedrich Sthamer-Gesellschaft. I had known Herr Sthamer when he was German Ambassador in England, in the difficult days after the War; and I had received many kindnesses at his hands, which I shall never forget. I knew something of the work which he did in the cause of a good understanding between England and Germany. He came from 'the parts about Hamburg'. (Many of us English, as I was reminded by some of my hearers, also came from those parts, about fifteen hundred years ago.) It is easy for an Englishman to feel at home in Hamburg. It was particularly easy for me to feel at home when I was speaking in Hamburg before a society which bears the name of Herr Sthamer....His son was present at my lecture....I cannot but inscribe to his name and his memory what I have written.

ERNEST BARKER

CAMBRIDGE
24 DECEMBER 1936

OLIVER CROMWELL AND THE ENGLISH PEOPLE

I

OLIVER CROMWELL has no grave. His dead body, dug up by the Royalists after the King came back, at the beginning of 1661, was hung and beheaded, and then thrown into a pit.[1] As he has no grave, so, until recent times, he has had no memorial. It was not until 1845 that the first great book was dedicated to his memory; and then it was dedicated by a Scotsman, Thomas Carlyle, who collected and elucidated, in three volumes, his letters and speeches. It was not until 1899 that a statue was at last erected in his honour at Westminster, under the shadow of our Houses of Parliament. In general recognition, he is a late-comer into our national house of fame. But he has come at last, free from the shadows by which he was long obscured, and visible in his own true lineaments. To-day we can interrogate him freely.

'What is your substance? Whereof are you made?'

What is his significance in English history? What is the cause for which he stands, and what are the elements of our national life which are embodied and incarnate in his memory?

He was born in the April of 1599, at the end of the reign of Queen Elizabeth, in the Eastern Counties of England, in a fen-land country which was the home of a deep and devout Protestantism. He had the genius of this country, and above all its religious temper, deep in his blood.[2] He was over forty-one when he first appeared on the stage of public events, as member for the town of Cambridge, in the Long Parliament

which met at the end of 1640. He died
eighteen years later, in the September of
1658, a little short of his sixtieth year. In
these eighteen years he had wrestled, in
Parliament and outside, with grave religious
and political problems: he had made himself a great soldier, and ridden from victory
to victory in nine long years of war, from
the middle of 1642 to the end of 1651; and
finally, for the last five years of his life, from
1653 to 1658, when he was already weary
and spent, he had carried on his shoulders
the general burden of government, as 'His
Highness the Protector of the Commonwealth of England, Scotland and Ireland'.
He had served his generation simultaneously
in the political parliament, the military camp
and the religious congregation. The last of
the three had always been his true home.
From that home he went out to war and
politics, and wherever he went he carried
its spirit with him. But military fame and
political power weighed with him as well as

religious faith: he was no pure saint, but a thunderer of war and a calculator of political expediencies mixed with a seeker who sought for God. In his mixed and comprehensive nature, which in the world of action was what Shakespeare's was in the world of literature, there were different and conflicting elements. His achievement is as various as himself, and it leaves room for different and conflicting interpretations.

II

Shall we interpret him as the maker of the unity of the United Kingdom; the author of unification; the creator of one *Reich* or *Respublica*, which transcended and abolished local particularisms, and embraced all the British Isles? In a sense he was. The Lord Protector governed a single *Respublica*, in the Parliament of which representatives of England, Scotland and Ireland sat together for the first time. There was a single citizen-

14

ship, a common constitution, a single system of trade, a common ordering of the
basis of religious life, through all its borders.
But this was not so much his own intention,
as the aftermath and consequence of a civil
war, in which all three countries had been
engaged, and which, ending in the victory
of one cause, necessarily ended in the en-
throning of that cause over all the three
countries. In any case—and this is the fundamental thing—the achievement did not
last. It perished within two years of his
death, when Charles II was restored to the
throne in 1660. Scotland and Ireland went
back to their old positions. If Scotland
afterwards consented to a Union, in 1707,
she consented to a voluntary and negotiated
union, which owed nothing to the memory
of Cromwell's experiment. If Ireland was
afterwards, long afterwards, brought into
a Union, in 1801, that union too was independent of his memory; and it has not
lasted. What Cromwell did in Scotland and

Ireland was written on wind and running water. The wind blew; the waters ran; and it went. Even the part of the Cromwellian settlement of Ireland which seemed most permanent—the planting of English land-lords on more than half of the soil of Ireland—is gone. It began to go in 1870, when the principle of land purchase, or in other words of the substitution of peasant proprietor-ship in lieu of tenancy, was introduced in favour of Irish tenants: it finally went in the first decade of the twentieth century.

III

Another interpretation of Cromwell would make him the author of colonial expansion and imperial policy—the arch-founder, if not the first begetter, of the British Empire. In these days of a conscious passion for colonial expansion this is a natural inter-pretation. We always tend to interpret the past in the light of the prepossessions which we cherish in the present; and when we idealize colonial expansion as a sign of national vigour, a symbol of national prestige, and an expression of national responsibility towards undeveloped peoples and regions, we are apt to project our ideals into the past. There is a sense in which the interpretation of Cromwell's achievement in colonial and imperial terms is correct. His Admiral Blake pushed into the Mediterranean, partly in pursuit of fugitive Royalists who had taken to privateering, partly to police the seas against the Algerian pirates, and partly to make a display of English naval strength which might overawe Catholic powers inimical to the English Protestant Republic. This was the beginning of a policy of the acquisition of Mediterranean power which was afterwards steadily pursued. Again there was Cromwell's war with Spain, which virtually began at the end of 1654 and lasted for the rest of his life. This may be viewed as a challenge to the great colonial empire of Spain; and it certainly resulted in the conquest of Jamaica, in the West Indies, during the summer of 1655. Nor is this all. During his ascendancy a common Puritanism—a common basis of Free Church feeling—cemented more closely the colonies of New England to the government of Old England. Again a new Navigation Law of 1651 (not, it is true, due to Cromwell, and resulting in a Dutch War which ran counter both to his religious feelings and to his political sympathies) practically reserved the commerce of English colonies for English shipping. There even seems to have been a conscious theory of the necessity of the expansion of England. The words of Harrington, a political theorist of Cromwell's time, may be cited. 'You cannot plant an oak in a flower pot: she must have earth for her roots, and heaven for her branches.'

All this is well worth noting; and it all seems to lead naturally to the view that

Cromwell, and Cromwell's England, were imperialists. But there are deep and cogent reasons against accepting such a simple and categorical explanation. Those reasons may be stated in one word—the word 'religion'. We must never forget that the England of the years in which Cromwell spent his active life—the England of the years 1620 to 1660—was an England in a great mood of religious exaltation. This exaltation was not a show or a cloak or an hypocrisy: it was the genuine spirit of the age. Moved by the influence of this spirit, the expansion of England was a religious expansion. This is apparent in two ways, different from one another, and yet complementary to one another. In the first place, the effective and permanent expansion of England—anterior to Cromwell, and beginning about 1620 in the form of Puritan emigration—was in no way due to political or 'geopolitical' reasons. It was not promoted by the State: it was undertaken from motives of religion in order to enable men to escape from the State and its policy of compulsory religious unity, and to find a religious haven or 'free port', like your own great port of Hamburg. 'The expansion of England in the seventeenth century was an expansion of society and not of the State. Society expanded to escape from the pressure of the State.'[3] In the second place, and in the days when, under Cromwell, the State began to take a hand, the State itself—the Puritan State of the period of the Commonwealth—was predominantly moved by considerations of religion. We should be committing treason against the spirit of the age, and we should be guilty of false history, if we did not recognize the dominance of these considerations. When Cromwell embarked on war against Spain in 1655 (and it is by this war, and not the earlier Dutch War, which was *not* his, that we must judge his motive), he was not acting on grounds of colonial expansion and imperial policy. The evidence may be found in his speech to Parliament, one of his longest, and the most curiously and deeply illuminated, of 17 September 1656. That speech has been cited by a German writer, Dr Carl Schmitt, in an essay on 'the conception of the political',[4] as a revealing illustration of the truth that the essence of 'the political' is the ability and the will to distinguish friend and foe, and highly to resolve on the negation of the foe. But the speech is not a speech in terms of 'the political', nor is it couched in the interest of the English State. It is a speech in terms of 'the religious', and it is couched in the interest of a common European Protestantism. The battle which Cromwell sees arrayed is not a battle of states, but a battle of faiths. It is true that he begins his speech by a frank confession of enmity: 'Why, truly, your great Enemy is the Spaniard.' But we begin to see into his mind as soon as he states the reasons and the ground of this enmity. The Spaniard is an enemy 'naturally, by that antipathy which is in him—and also providentially'. That word 'providentially', as Carlyle justly interprets it, means 'by special ordering of Providence'. It is the Providence of God which has put an enmity between the true religion and the religion which is not true, and therefore between the Englishman and the Spaniard. Nor is the true religion the cause or the interest of England only. 'All the honest interests; yea, all interests of the Protestants, in Germany, Denmark, Helvetia and the Cantons, and all the interests in Christendom, are the same as yours. If you succeed...and be convinced what is God's Interest, and prosecute it, you will find that you act for a very great many who are God's own.' It is therefore for 'God's Interest', and 'all the interests in Christendom', that Cromwell would have England stand. Not but what he feels (for it would be wrong to blink the truth or to deny some national prejudice) that England

22

has some sort of special right or special duty
to act. 'We are Englishmen: that is one
good fact; and if God give a nation the property of valour and courage, it is honour
and a mercy from Him.' But having made
that confession, he adds at once, in his very
next words: 'And much more than English!
Because you all, I hope, are Christian Men,
who know Jesus Christ, and know that
Cause.'

Men's motives are always mixed. If religion shone in the forefront of Cromwell's
mind, it would be folly to deny that mixed
motives of Mars and Mammon—military
and naval glory, territorial conquest and expansion, the profit of trade and commerce
—were operative in the background. English Puritanism in general was something of
a Midas, turning what it touched into gold,
as well as an Antigone, resolved to obey at
any cost the commandments of God. Oliver
himself could say to his Council in 1654:
'Having 160 ships swimming...we think

our best consideration had to keep us this reputation and improve it for some good, and not lay them up by the walls.... This design would cost little more than laying by the ships, and that with hope of great profit.'[5] Again, if Cromwell could ejaculate, with a genuine passion, 'And much more than English!', he could also believe, as John Milton had said in his *Areopagitica* in 1644, that when 'God is decreeing to begin some great and new period in his Church ...what does he then but reveal himself to his servants, and as his manner is first to his Englishmen?' There *was* a kind of Hebraic exclusive nationalism in the Puritans (after all, their minds were fed on the reading of the Old Testament); and though it had a religious basis, and could, in virtue of that basis, show a generous European side, it was apt to become, at the best an idealized, and at the worst a commercialized patriotism. Professor Trevelyan has justly said that 'the Protector's mind could never logically separate this idealized patriotism from his Protestant and Free Church sympathies'.[6] Perhaps even we, three hundred years later, cannot make such a logical separation. The currents of this world are not always corrupted; but they are seldom, if ever, unmixed.

IV

When all is said, and when all allowances have been made, it remains impossible to explain the achievement of Cromwell in any simple political terms, whether of the unification of the United Kingdom, or of colonial expansion and imperial policy, or of both. The unification and the expansion were both incidental: they were both by-products, naturally enough thrown out, of great motions of the human mind and the stirring of great events which had other intentions and purposes. Those motions, and that stirring, had produced two Civil Wars, which lasted from the summer of 1642 to the autumn of 1651. In the course of these Civil Wars two things, both unprojected and unforeseen, had happened. In the first place all the three countries—England, Scotland and Ireland—had been involved. The end of the struggle necessarily entailed a new settlement of their relations; and that settlement, which was not originally in debate, but had been afterwards drawn into debate, was necessarily made, as has already been said, by the victor in debate, and necessarily made on the basis of a unified system, congruous with his own ecclesiastical and political ideas. It was an inevitable result; but it was as unintended as it was inevitable, and it proved to be as temporary as it was unintended. In the second place the Civil Wars, in the course of their long duration, had raised questions of foreign policy—questions of the relations of the British Isles to other Powers and the outer world. There had been threats of intervention during the wars; there was still the fear of intervention when they ended. Moreover, they had produced a military and a naval force unparalleled before in our history, and unparalleled for long years afterwards—a drilled and disciplined army, which numbered 60,000 foot, horse and dragoons by the beginning of the Protectorate; and a navy vastly increased in strength and vastly improved in the quality of its officers and men. Fear was thus backed by force; and fear and force, guided by a religious crusading sentiment which was curiously mixed with an Hebraic nationalism (itself mixed, in its turn, with calculations of territorial conquest and commercial gain), issued in war with Spain. But this again was an aftermath and a by-product in the history of the Puritan Revolution and in the evolution of Oliver Cromwell. It was not an original part of the great struggle of his public life. It came at the end, in the winter of his years; and this is one of the cases in which we cannot judge by the end. We shall judge him better if we remember that at the end of the first Civil War, in the winter of 1646–1647, he was seriously thinking of leaving England, with such soldiers as he could gather, to fight with the German Calvinists in the Thirty Years War.

V

This brings us back to the real core of Cromwell's achievement and his essential significance in the history of his country. He was the incarnation—perhaps the greatest we have had—of the genius of English Nonconformity, which is the peculiar and (it may even be said) the cardinal factor in the general development of English politics and English national life. He was the expression of the great Free Church movement which runs through our modern history, and therefore, fundamentally—because the two things are intimately and irrevocably interconnected—he was also the expression of what I would call the

28

great Free State movement which also runs through our history. This is a deep and solemn thesis, which demands explanation; which needs qualification; but which, in the last resort and the general account, commands its own justification

When Cromwell appeared on the scene, at the end of 1641, the current and dominant notion in England was the notion that a single political society was, and ought to be, a single religious society. It was a notion inherited from the Middle Ages, with the one difference that, while the Middle Ages had believed that a single *universal* political society involved a single universal religious society, seventeenth-century England believed that a single *national* political society involved a single national religious society. This was, in effect, a doctrine of religious territorialism. We may also call it a doctrine of the equivalence of *populus*, *respublica* and *ecclesia*; or, if we prefer the English terms used by Hooker, a doctrine of the equivalence of people, commonwealth and Church; or, if we use German terms, a doctrine of the equivalence of *Volk*, *Staat* and *Kirche*. Now in 1641 there were two schools of opinion which both accepted this doctrine, but none the less differed from one another. There were the Anglicans, who believed that all England should be a single Anglican Church, episcopally governed, and following a modified form of the old medieval ritual. There were the Presbyterians or Calvinists, who believed that all England should be a single Presbyterian Church, governed by presbyteries and synods of presbyteries, and following the new ritual of Geneva. These two schools, differing in spite of their common premiss, not only differed on religious issues: they also differed in politics. The Anglicans, who found room for the King, in the system of episcopal government, as the supreme governor of the Church, were Royalists. The Presbyterians, who found

room for a General Assembly, in the system
of Presbyterian government, as the final
authority of the Church, were Parliamentarians. But between them both, or over
and above them both, there remained a
tertium quid. This was the Independents;
in other words, the members of the Free
Churches; in other words again—to mention their two great main varieties—the
Congregationalists and the Baptists. The
essence of their position was that they
denied what I have called the doctrine of
equivalence, which was accepted both by
the Anglicans and the Presbyterians. They
did *not* believe that a single political society
was, or ought to be, a single religious
society. They did *not* profess the doctrine
of religious territorialism. They were essentially and literally Nonconformists. They
believed that any voluntary society of
Christian men and women, in any area or
neighbourhood in which they were gathered
together, should be free to form their own

congregation and to constitute their own Free Church.

This was a cardinal tenet which lay at the heart of Cromwell's thought, and vitally affected the development of England during his lifetime and for generations afterwards. It had large and general consequences. One of these consequences was the idea and practice of the limited State. According to this tenet, a political society had not the right to require and impose the pattern of a single religious society, corresponding to its own image, or to demand a uniform system of ecclesiastical government and religious ritual. Liberty of conscience and liberty of worship were fundamentals; and no human authority could defeat them or abridge them. This was a great and pregnant consequence; and it might, and it ultimately did, widen out further issues—the issue, for example, of free trade, or again that of free labour, to both of which something of a religious consecration came to be attached by virtue of the original and seminal idea of the Free Church.[7] So great, and so potent, was the genius of Independent Non-Conformity. But there was also another consequence of the cardinal tenet of the Free Church. This was the idea and practice of the democratic State, dependent on the principle of free association, and based on the deliberate thought of all its members, collected by due process of discussion and reduced, by that process, to the unity of a common sense. If the Independents did not desire a Church after the image of the State, they came to require a State after the image of the Church—that is to say, of their own Free Church. Just as the religious congregation was to be freely constituted and governed, and to wait upon God until it discovered the common 'sense of the meeting' and thereby knew His way of righteousness, so the political association was also to be freely constituted and governed, and it too was to wait on the movement of the human spirit, going this way and that in discussion, until it too discovered a common sense and thereby knew the way of human justice and peace.

VI

These were ideas which seethed in the mind of Cromwell and the minds of his brother-Independents, and which they sought to realize in the hour of victory—in the years from 1653 to 1658, when both the Anglican Royalists, who stood for episcopacy and the divine right of the King, and the Presbyterian Parliamentarians, who stood for presbyteries and the sovereign right of a small and exclusive Parliament, had been defeated by the issue of the two Civil Wars. But that very phrase, 'the hour of victory', reveals a great paradox in the history of the Independents, which was also the paradox of Cromwell's life and achievement. In its very nature the cause of the Free Church is not victorious, and has no hour of victory;

it is a protest and a challenge to an alien majority. It is the cause of a struggling minority—protesting, challenging, resisting. It is the cause of an Antigone, face to face with Creon and his edicts. When Antigone becomes Creon—when the resister himself is armed with the powers and resources of the State—there is an inherent paradox, or rather dualism, in his position. This dualism or paradox becomes all the more evident when we reflect that the strength of Cromwell, and of his Independent adherents, lay from first to last in the army. Cromwell began his effective career as a colonel of cavalry. He became, in 1645, Lieutenant-General of the whole army opposed to the King: he became, in 1650, its General. He was an army leader, carried by the army on its shoulders into control when the army became, at the end of the wars, the residuary victor in the struggle—when the King had been executed, in January 1649, and when the small and exclusive Parlia-

35 3-2

ment, which stood for its privilege no less stiffly than the King for his prerogative, had been evicted in April 1653. It is true that the army was a remarkable and unparalleled army; and that in two ways. Largely under the influence of Cromwell, who when he first began to raise a troop of cavalry had insisted on having around him honest God-fearing men, it was an army penetrated through and through by the spirit of Independency—an army which assembled in meeting for prayer on the eve of any great issue, and would stop to sing a short Psalm even in the heat and passion of battle.[8] It was also an army penetrated by a democratic spirit—an army which held itself to be a great primary assembly of the people as well as a great congregation of the faithful. It had known, in its day, what we should nowadays call soviets of soldiers (they were then called Agitators or Agents of the regiments): it continued to know debates, projects of constitutions, discus-

sions of Englishmen's rights and duties.
...But it was an army none the less. It gave
its General a world of trouble. But he was
its General; and he held it together as long
as he lived.

This standing Free Church army (not all
Free Church, for in its early days it had contained a number of pressed or conscripted
soldiers, and in its later days it contained a
number who followed the wars as an ordinary profession; but still predominantly
Free Church) is a standing curiosity in our
history, as its memory was a standing fear
to later generations. Normally our Free
Churches have stood away from the army:
normally our army has stood in connection
with the Crown and the Established Church,
to which it then stood opposed. But these
were revolutionary times; and this army was
a revolutionary, and therefore abnormal,
thing. It was a wedding of two different
ideals—the ideal of the voluntary life in
things temporal as well as spiritual: the

ideal of the life which is schooled, regimented and drilled. The army in which these ideals were wedded believed in a free England, the home of free churchmanship and corresponding free citizenship; and yet it was constrained to hold England down by virtue of its very beliefs. After all it was a minority. In that it was true to the general genius of its cause, which in the general run of our history has been the cause of a struggling minority. But it was a minority which for the time being held the sword, and possessed might, majesty, dominion and power. It faced the majority boldly, but with a division in its heart, enforcing liberty, and yet disbelieving in force. The contradiction could not last; and it did not last. But there was nothing ignoble, and nothing common or mean, in all the contradiction, and all the wrestlings and strivings, which vexed in their hour of victory the general body of Independents, the Independent army which was their core, and 'the great

Independent', Oliver the Protector (not unfitly so called), who was summoned by a heavy and exacting destiny to reconcile the principles of the cause he led with the urgent needs of national healing and settling.

VII

The sole and ultimate responsibility of Cromwell, and the great period of his life by which his achievement and significance must ultimately be judged, belong to the five and a half years which lie between the eviction of Parliament in April 1653 and his death in September 1658.[9] True, he had been the dynamic and driving force for at least half a dozen years earlier, in every crisis of events. If any man won the war against the Royalists, it was he. If any man was responsible for the execution of the King, it was he. If any man left a mark upon Ireland—and a cruel mark at that—it was he. But the real test came when—the war won, the King dead, Ireland and Scotland reduced, and Parliament finally evicted—he and his army stood, at last, face to face with the final burden of decision. Fighting was over: the time for the short, sharp shrift of the sword was gone: the time had come for facing an opposition in peace, and by the methods of peace. The opposition was numerous—far more numerous than the government—and though it was various and divided, its different sections were gradually beginning to coalesce. On the extreme Right stood the Royalists and Anglicans: on the moderate Right (but still on the Right) there were some who were Presbyterian Parliamentarians, and some who were plain Parliamentarians, clinging to the notion of a traditional and historic constitution of which an historic Parliament was a necessary and essential ingredient. The Right in general, which carried with it the instincts of the country, was the side of civilianism in the face of military rule: it was the side of traditionalism; it was also, because that was part of the tradition, the side of religious uniformity. But there was also a Left, which went far beyond Cromwell and the main body of the Independents. There were political Levellers, or Radicals, who had a passion for the sovereignty of the people, manhood suffrage, the natural rights of man, and the whole of the full-fledged doctrine of revolutionary democracy which emerged in France in 1789. There were also the social Levellers—men who would be called to-day Communists, but who confined their communism, as was natural in an agrarian age, to an attack on property in land, and to the assertion that 'the Earth is the Lord's, not particular men's who claim a proper interest in it above others'. The social Levellers were few; but in raising the issue of private property, and in pressing it against the general and captains of the Independent army, they brought out a fact which must not be forgotten. Cromwell and the men with whom he worked were themselves, in many respects, innovators and radicals. But on the point of property they too were traditional and conservative. The doctrine of the Free Churches did not entail any social programme, or any new distribution of property.

In the face of this opposition Cromwell stood, first and foremost, as he had always stood, for religious liberty. He stood for the idea and practice of the limited State, which did not enforce religious uniformity, but was bound by the 'fundamental' of respecting Christian freedom of conscience and Christian freedom of worship. This meant an ensured and guaranteed toleration, obligatory on the State, and superior to the State, which thus became, under the compulsion of an overriding principle of religious liberty, the home of varied forms of belief living in a common peace and interacting on one another in a mutual influence. But the toleration which was thus to proceed from the nature of a limited State was a toleration sadly and drastically limited in its own nature. Bound by the spirit of their own belief, which would only recognize as 'true religion' the Protestant form of religion, and only the more Protestant form of that form, Cromwell and his associates in the Free Churches could not tolerate Anglicanism, and far less Roman Catholicism. Both Prelacy and Popery lay beyond the pale. This was a large and sweeping exception to the principle of religious liberty—so large and so sweeping that it may seem, at any rate to our own age, to negate the principle. We have to remember that the initial range of the application of any principle is small, and will gradually grow with the benefit of time and the widening of men's minds. We have equally to remember that this principle, when it was enunciated, was a radical principle, and a flat contradiction of the current doctrine of the equivalence of people, commonwealth and church. The fundamental principle, in spite of the sad and drastic exceptions to its application, is that a man may freely hold his belief, and freely celebrate his worship, according to the motion of his spirit, and that no earthly authority may interfere with that motion. Cromwell, like Luther, had a firm hold of the idea of the liberty of the Christian man in the inner springs of his life; and that idea carried him even farther than Luther, because it lead him to deny, as Luther never did, the doctrine of religious territorialism—the doctrine of the equivalence of political and religious society. 'Truly, these things do respect the souls of men, and the spirits, which are the men. The mind is the man.'[10] He had stood for this idea in the first Civil War. 'For brethren, in things of the mind', he had written to Parliament in 1645, 'we look for no compulsion, but that of light and reason'. He had stood for it in the second Civil War. 'I desire from my heart', he

wrote in 1648, 'I have prayed for...union
and right understanding between the godly
people—Scots, English, Jews, Gentiles,
Presbyterians, Anabaptists, and all.'[11] He
stood for it still in the system he created in
the days of his power and Protectorate.
Religious funds and endowments were used
for the common benefit of the Presbyterian
clergy and of the Independent clergy of the
Congregationalist and Baptist varieties. By
the side of the clergy paid from these funds
and endowments there also existed clergy,
of whatever variety or denomination, sup-
ported by the free offerings of their own
voluntary congregations. The Quakers
were a notable example of such voluntary
congregations; but the sects were numerous
in these tumultuous times. Even the Anglicans sometimes met, illegally but by con-
nivance, for public worship; and though
even that was denied to the Roman
Catholics, there was no other persecution
of their belief, nor were they dragooned

into attendance at alien forms of worship by fine and punishment, as had been the case under the previous law of England.

In this qualified form there was, under Cromwell, a brief summer of religious liberty—not improperly so called when we remember the period of compulsory religious uniformity which preceded it, and the similar period which followed it when King and Church and Parliament were restored in 1660. This summer had abiding fruits. Thanks to Cromwell, as one of his biographers has said, 'Nonconformity had time to take root and to grow so strong in England that the storm which followed the Restoration had no power to root it up'.[12] English Nonconformity, with its doctrine of the limited State, and its aspiration towards a religious liberty which might become also a liberty in other spheres, continued to be a salt ingredient of English life, which maintained its peculiar savour and produced some of its most vital characteristics.

VIII

Religious liberty is a great thing; but there is also political liberty. It was said above that there were two consequences involved in the cardinal tenet of Independency. One of them was the idea and practice of the limited State—the State limited by the principle of religious liberty: the other was the idea and practice of the democratic State—the State based on the principle of free association and free discussion. It is plain that Cromwell stood for religious liberty and the limited State: can it also be said that he stood for political liberty and the democratic State? We must frankly confess that in Cromwell's view, as his biographer has justly said, 'religious freedom was more important than political freedom'.[13] Religion stood in the forefront of his thought. But that is not to say that he had no passion for any liberty other than religious liberty. There is one of his speeches, brief but pregnant, of April 3, 1657, which lets us into his mind. He speaks of 'the two greatest concernments that God hath in the world'. 'The one is that of religion, and of the just preservation of all the professors of it; to give them all due and just Liberty.' This he calls 'the more peculiar interest of God', or 'the Interest of Christians'. The other is 'the Civil Liberty and Interest of the Nation'. This is subordinate to 'the Interest of Christians'; 'yet it is the next best God hath given men in this world'. It is also congruous with it: 'if any think the Interest of Christians and the Interest of the Nation inconsistent, or two different things, I wish my soul may never enter into their secrets....' 'And upon these two interests...I shall live and die....If I were asked, why I have engaged all along in the late war, I could give no answer that were not a wicked one if it did not comprehend these two ends.'

48

These are words—noble words—but what did he actually do? In the first place, he clung to the idea of the sovereignty of a written constitution—the constitution contained in the Instrument of Government, which had been produced, at the end of 1653, by the officers of the army. *Prima facie*, a constitution produced by the officers of an army, though it may be called an instrument of government, can hardly appear to be an instrument of political liberty. Moreover, in a country which had just emerged from a civil war originally waged in the name of the sovereign rights of Parliament, a constitution not produced by parliament, and overriding the rights of all subsequent parliaments, may well seem unconstitutional. These things are true enough; and Cromwell was to experience their truth in the course of his struggles with Parliament. But there are also other things which are true. The army which produced the constitution, through the agency of its officers, held itself to be a great primary assembly of the people; and by a section of the people, though only by a section, it *was* held to be such an assembly. But much more fundamental is the fact that the constitution, however produced, was a check and a limit, not only upon any parliament which subsequently assembled, but also upon Cromwell. It was a check and a limit which he voluntarily embraced and steadily upheld. It was indeed a check and limit which stood in lieu of the consent of the people, freely given and freely renewed. That could not be had, when the bulk of the nation stood in opposition, whether to the Right or Left. The written constitution was only a second best—a substitute for national consent. But at any rate it was something; and the idea struggling behind it, if not expressed in it—the idea of the sovereignty of a constitution made and accepted by the nation—was an idea in the true logic of genuine Independency.

In the second place, limited as he already was by a written constitution, Cromwell sought also to limit himself by the need of collaboration with Parliament. True, he had evicted a parliament—the old Parliament of the Civil Wars—at the beginning of the period of his own immediate rule. But the Parliament which he evicted had become a narrow civilian oligarchy; and two months after its eviction, even before the Instrument of Government had been evolved with its scheme of regular parliaments, he summoned a new parliament himself. After the adoption of the Instrument, two parliaments sat; and one of them held two sessions. They were not freely constituted parliaments: even so, they disagreed with Cromwell, and he with them; and they went their way. He was not a great parliamentarian; but neither was he an autocrat. After all, he had been a Member of Parliament himself, as the representative of Cambridge, from 1640 to 1653; and he never forgot this side of himself. He never deserted the forum entirely for the camp: he lived in both, and that was a great part of his greatness. He tried to live with parliament, to work with parliament, to reconcile an historic and traditional parliamentary system with the spirit of the Free Churches and the fact of a Free Church army. He did not succeed; but he did not desist from endeavour. He was at once inside and outside the main current of English history which makes for the sovereignty of Parliament—partly a soldier, and partly a civilian; partly a doctrinaire of the written constitution which aimed at setting religious liberty above the reach of parliament, and partly a parliament man.

But there was always a deep trend of his nature which drew him to the side of liberty—civil and political as well as religious. He was a man of a natural vitality and vivacity—'of such a vivacity', says a contemporary, 'as another man is when he hath drunken a cup of wine too much'. He carried himself easily among his fellows: he had, says the same contemporary, 'familiar rustic carriage with his soldiers in sporting'.[14] He did not speak much, it was noted, but he had a gift for making others speak. These are only externals; but they are externals which suggest a free spirit, able and ready to move in free intercourse with others. The trend of his inward nature led him towards a deep feeling for the free motion of the free spirit. There was a sect of his time who were called 'Seekers', because they believed in the need of perpetual search for truth. He had a sympathy for them. 'To be a Seeker', he once wrote, 'is to be of the best sect next after a finder, and such an one shall every faithful humble Seeker be in the end.' This may remind us of a saying of Jesus, in a papyrus found in Egypt over thirty years ago: 'Let not him that seeketh cease till he find, and when he findeth he shall wonder, and having wondered he shall reign, and having reigned he shall rest.'[15] Seeking; finding; wondering; reigning; resting—these words are, in a sense, an epitome of Cromwell's earthly course. But it is the word 'seeking' which is peculiarly characteristic. It suggests indeed one of his defects, to which I shall have to recur at the end—his habit of seeking and waiting for some visible 'evidence' from God, which made him an opportunist ready to identify the lead of events with the march of God's own providence. But it also suggests a great quality. He believed in the seeking mind. 'The mind is the man. If that be kept pure, a man signifies somewhat.' He believed that it was man's own business to keep the mind free. He held that it was 'an unjust and unwise jealousy to deprive a man of his natural liberty upon a supposition he may abuse it: when he *doth* abuse it, judge.' This implies, fundamentally, a grasp of the principle of what we may call *civil* liberty; and though there were civil liberties which, as we shall see, he restricted, the restrictions grew less as he himself gained a freer hand, towards the close of his Protectorate, and was less tied by the control of the officers of his army. In the same way—and this is a still more important matter—Cromwell's belief in the seeking mind led him to grasp the principle of *political* liberty. We must all seek together: we must all bring together the results of our seeking; and then we must discuss together the results which we have found. This is a conception which he had already attained by the autumn of 1647, after the end of the first Civil War, and which he expressed in the earnest debates on the future of England which were then being held in the victorious army. Not only is he clear that any plan for the future of England must be such that 'the spirits and temper of the nation are prepared to receive and go along with it'—a condition which, though he apprehended it, he failed himself in the event to satisfy—but he is also clear that any plan must be framed in the give and take of free discussion. This too was a condition which he failed in the event to satisfy. But it was none the less a condition which he had apprehended and never forgot. What a philosophic student of the debates of 1647 has written is fundamentally true. 'What Cromwell has learned from his experience of the small democracy of the Christian congregation, is the insight into the purposes of life which the common life and discussion of a democratic society can give.... This is his position—toleration and recognition of differences...combined with insistence that individual views shall submit to the criticism of open discussion.'[16]

But he was doomed to find that discussion was too difficult an art to practise, for the simple reason that toleration and recognition of differences were not present. The conflicting views conflicted too much to submit to mutual criticism or to be recon-

ciled by the process of discussion. There is a
story that Cromwell, on the night of the
execution of Charles I, came to look at the
face of his dead king, and as he looked
sighed out the words, 'Cruel Necessity'.
Cruel Necessity was always upon him. He
wrestles with this notion of Necessity sadly
in his speech of 17 September 1656. There
has been, he confesses, for some time a
military rule of different parts of England
by Major-Generals: there has been what he
somewhat mildly terms 'a keeping of some
in prison'; there have been other things—
'*which, we say, was Necessity*'. He knows that
this is a dangerous plea: 'I confess, if Necessity be pretended, that is so much the more
sin', but he pleads it none the less, as 'a man
of honest heart, engaged to God', who is
lifted above pretension, and is only acting
under dire and real compulsion. He pleads
Necessity the more readily because the
notion of it, as a thing sent and imposed by
God, is mixed in his mind with another

notion—the notion of Reformation, or, as he calls it, 'Reformation of Manners'. The people have sinned and gone astray: they must be recalled to God and the way of righteousness. Here the cause of Independency and the theory of the Free Church twists round, as it were, in the hands of its authors. It loses its edge of freedom: it begins to show a stern and sharp edge of compulsion, as of 'the sword of the Lord and of Gideon'. After all (we must always remember) the cause of Independency was also the cause of an army—a drilled and disciplined army, ready to impose drill and discipline on others as well as itself. This was the paradox or dualism always inherent in Independency and in the mind of 'the great Independent' who led its cause. On the one hand freedom, and no compulsion in things of the mind. On the other hand an Old Testament passion for reformation, like that of the Hebrew prophets...and behind this passion an army.

Two notions—the notion of Reformation, and the notion of Necessity—thus conspired against the notion of civil and political liberty. Necessity imposed arbitrary taxes, called 'decimations', on the property of Royalists. Necessity and Reformation combined instituted the system of the twelve Major-Generals, in twelve districts of England, who were charged both to repress political enemies and to suppress immorality. Civil liberty was restricted by the restriction of ale-houses and race-meetings. Political liberty was equally restricted by the same restrictions. Ale-houses and race-meetings were dangerous because the disaffected, and especially the Royalists, might meet there to discuss their grievances and to ventilate their criticisms. The political philosophy of Cromwell thus yielded to political exigency. He who had insisted, in the army debates of the autumn of 1647, 'that individual views shall submit to the criticism of open discussion' was within a decade stifling criticism and preventing open discussion. He did not suppress the central parliament; but there was a period—the period of these Major-Generals, who lasted from the autumn of 1655 to the spring of 1657—during which he suppressed the local discussion that sustains and underlies an effective central parliament. It was a period during which, on one occasion, he even 'swore roundly' at Magna Charta itself—the traditional palladium of English liberties, in the name of which Parliament had originally resisted Charles I. The best that can be said for Cromwell is that the period was transitory. It ended with the abolition of the Major-Generals in the spring of 1657. The last year and a half of Cromwell's life, from the spring of 1657 to the autumn of 1658, was a period of the decline of military power; of return to the civilian tradition of English life; of closer, if still imperfect, collaboration with parliament; of less of the twin causes of Necessity and Reformation, and more of the cause of the Civil Liberty and 'Interest of the Nation'. We do not know what this period would have been if it had lasted. It did not last. Cromwell died.

IX

He was a man contrary in some respects to our English tradition. The written constitution for which he stood; the standing army which he led; the compulsory reformation of manners which, at one period, he sought—these are all alien from our permanent trend. But in one great thing, which is greater than all these, he was fundamentally true to the English genius—or rather to one side of that genius, which is not the whole, but is none the less an integral part and essential characteristic of the whole. He was, and is, beyond any other man, the expression of English Nonconformity, alike in its qualities and its defects: the reflection of its idea of the primacy of religious liberty, its idea of the limited State, its idea of the State based on free association and proceeding by free discussion. He was not, indeed, a true reflection in all that he did or all that he was. The time-mirror was too distorting: the limitations of his age, and the contingencies of contemporary events, made the reflection of religious liberty pale and thin, and that of political liberty dwarfed and stunted. But with all its imperfections the reflection stands, and will continue to stand, whenever we look at his face and lineaments.

Was he also characteristic of the English genius in another sense? A German writer on England, Professor Dibelius, has said that the mutations of our history have always the result 'of giving fuller scope for leadership'. 'Wherever the Englishman scents a leader, he always bows before him.'[17] Was Cromwell an example of our English passion for leadership? It would be hard to maintain that thesis.[18] Leadership, he deeply felt, came from God, showing itself in the 'evidences' He gave and the 'providences' He vouchsafed: it was simply his business to follow. The ordinary metaphor which he used of himself was the humble metaphor of a constable, keeping the peace, as it were, in the streets. 'His work was to keep several judgments in peace, because, like men falling out in the streets, they would run their heads one against another; he was as a constable to part them and keep them in peace.' This was a saying of the year 1655: it was repeated in a speech to Parliament of 13 April 1657: 'I could not tell what my business was, nor what I was in the place I stood in, save comparing myself to a good constable set to keep the peace of a parish.' The figure of Cromwell, as he saw it himself, is that of a homely English policeman—a policeman tired and weary, who 'would have lived under his woodside, to have kept a flock of sheep, rather than undertake such a government as this is.'[19] He did not regard himself as a leader; nor was he so regarded even by his own associates. Opposed by all who were not Independents, he was also compelled to wrestle with the Independents themselves; and the way which he eventually went, even to the very end, and even when he was more free from the political control of the army than he had ever been before, was the way which his officers pressed upon him rather than his own way. The history of the Commonwealth and Protectorate is not the history of Cromwell's leadership. There was always debate and discussion, tussle and compromise, even if it were confined to the limited circle of the Independents. The habit of the Independents was always a habit of congregationalism. Even the Independent army debated, because it was a congregation as well as an army. Cromwell was Cromwell, and he out-topped his contemporaries. But there were men of iron and deep speech by his side; and the action which he and they took was always collegiate action.

Common to most of these men, but peculiarly deep in Cromwell, was the conviction of Divine leadership. He, above all of them, was always seeking, by 'the dark lantern of the spirit', for evidences of the providential intentions and overrulings of God. To himself he was a man who was led—led by the hand—led through the wilderness. He was always waiting for the leader's hand. This stamped him, in the memory of many generations afterwards, as the consummate hypocrite. 'He lived a hypocrite and died a traitor', wrote one of our English poets a hundred years ago.[20] But his only hypocrisy, if it can be called such, was an overreadiness to throw the cloak of Divine intention and agency over his human acts. This was not a deception of others: it was a deception of himself, and a deception honestly practised. We must remember the mental world in which he lived—a world of predestined happenings, in which the moving finger of God was always writing the script. He always lived in that world: he always waited on the moving finger. The word 'waiting' recurs in his language; and this waiting and attendance on Providence—this expectation that God will provide, and this holding back for His time—slips readily into a sort of opportunism which is easily misinterpreted. 'I am one of those whose heart God hath drawn out to wait for some extraordinary dispensations.' 'Let us look into providences: surely they mean somewhat: they so hang together.' 'This hath been the way God hath dealt with us all along; to keep things from our eyes all along, so that we have seen nothing in all His dispensations long beforehand—which is also a witness, in some measure, to our integrity.' 'Sir, what can be said of these things?...It is

66

the Lord only.... Sir, you see the work is done by a Divine leading.'[21]

It is a dangerous doctrine—this doctrine of a Divine leading. It consecrates; but it consecrates too indiscriminately. It was the source of Cromwell's strength; but it was also the source of his weakness. It enabled him to hide the exigencies and the calculations of politics behind a plea of the intentions of God. It enabled a man who loved mercy to practise sometimes a sad cruelty: it enabled a man who loved liberty to allege the necessity of oppression: it enabled a man who believed in open discussion to silence its play. If this was not hypocrisy, it was at any rate self-contradiction; and this self-contradiction was inherent in himself and in the cause which he championed. Perhaps it is also inherent in the English people—the English people at large, in its general historical career, and not merely the section of the English people for whom Cromwell stood, in the middle of the seventeenth century. If that be so, then Cromwell is typical indeed: he reflects not only English Nonconformity, but also the whole of England, in its mingled composition of strength and weakness, good and evil. It is hard for an Englishman to judge. We cannot see ourselves as others see us. Cromwell himself thought the English 'the best people in the world'. That, it must be confessed, sounds a very English saying. But he only thought them best if there was present in them, and when there was present in them, another people —'the people of God', a people ready to serve Him and follow Him faithfully.[22] He could believe, more readily than we can to-day, that such another people was actually present in the English people. We, at a later age, can only long, and pray, that it may be present.

X

There is one thing for which all Englishmen
can admire Cromwell. When his thought ran
clear, in its rare moments of distillation, he
could write and speak English which moves
the heart in the same way as Shakespeare's
English. He often struggled in tortuous
sentences and involved periods. But sometimes he speaks out like a man; and then his
speech shows his stature. His last prayer,
uttered a few days before he died, is unforgettable: 'I may, I will, come to Thee, for
Thy People.... Lord, however Thou do dis-
pose of me, continue and go on to do good
for them. Give them consistency of judgment, one heart, and mutual love; and go
on to deliver them, and with the work of
reformation; and make the Name of Christ
glorious in the world.... And pardon the
folly of this short Prayer, even for Jesus
Christ's sake. And give us a good night, if
it be Thy pleasure. Amen.' Unforgettable

words. So, too, are some other words, which may fitly conclude this account of his thoughts and achievements. 'Let us all be not careful what men will make of these actings. They, will they, nill they, shall fulfil the good pleasure of God, and we shall serve our generations. Our rest we expect elsewhere: that will be durable.'[23]

The writer would ask the reader's indulgence if, in the Epilogue which follows, some themes or quotations, already handled or used, are again repeated. The repetition is intentional; but it is perhaps also inartistic.

EPILOGUE

The English Puritan Revolution and the German National Socialist Revolution

I

In Germany to-day the figure of Oliver Cromwell stands massively present in the mind and imagination of many. He has become the type of English character and achievement. He is 'the founder of the English fleet' and 'the author of the expansion of England'. These are exaggerations or misconceptions. The herrings of the North Sea had more to do with the founding of the English fleet than any man: if any man can be credited with its founding, the man was Henry VIII rather than Oliver Cromwell; and so far as the navy was cherished and extended in Oliver's time (as it was in the years which immediately followed the death of Charles I), the merit was not his, but belonged to the Presbyterian Parliament, which encouraged the more innocuous sailor as a counterblast to the Independent soldier. The expansion of England owes more to Cromwell; but his conquest of Jamaica was a much smaller factor in that expansion than the earlier Puritan colonization of New England, and Cromwell's policy of encouraging the Puritan settlers in New England to move southwards again to Jamaica was a policy calculated rather to hinder than to help the growth of his country's colonial power. He was more true to the natural genius of English expansion when he himself thought, as a good tradition suggests that he did, about 1630, of emigrating to New England in the wake of the East Anglian exodus which had begun about 1628.

But there is a deeper reason why Cromwell should present himself to Germany to-day as a remarkable and arresting figure. Historical parallels are often dubious; and to draw a parallel between an Englishman, living in a period and a century of the dominance of the religious motive, and a German who lives and moves in a period and an epoch of the dominance of social and economic motives, is especially difficult and especially dubious. But to draw an historical parallel is itself an historical fact, which may have historical influence; and whatever the justice or the propriety of the parallel, the fact and the influence must be taken into our reckoning. There *is* a sense in which the English Puritan Revolution of the seventeenth century and the German National Socialist Revolution of recent years have their analogies. Cromwell came upon an England which was bitterly divided in regard to the ultimate foundations of national life. Monarchism quarrelled with parliamentarianism; both of them quarrelled with incipient democratic doctrines of the sovereignty of the people, and even with incipient communistic doctrines of the ownership of the people's land: Anglicanism, Presbyterianism and Independency jostled together. For a time, if only for a time, Cromwell gave unity: he drew his country together, in a common 'assimilation' to a dominant trend: he insisted on a common foundation of common 'fundamentals'. In the same way, it may be said, the leader of National Socialism came upon a Germany which was equally divided: in the same way he drew his country together: in the same way he insisted on a unity of fundamentals.

The parallel may be carried further. If we look at the field of foreign relations, we may say that Cromwell, succeeding to the vacillating policy of the Stuart kings, gave England a new self-respect and a new prestige in the councils of Europe; and we may equally say that the leader of National Socialism, also succeeding to a previous period of vacillation, gave the same gifts to his people. But perhaps the parallel is closest when we turn to the field of what Cromwell called 'the reformation of manners'. This was the field in which, above all, he felt himself called to labour. His last prayer was a prayer that his people might have 'consistency of judgment, one heart and mutual love': a prayer to God to 'go on to deliver them, and with the work of reformation'. The leader of National Socialism has equally looked to the work of reformation. At its worst, reformation has meant for him anti-Semitism, the isolation of opponents in concentration camps ('a keeping of some in prison', as Cromwell put it), and the sharp and terrible purge of the midsummer of 1934. But there is a speech of 28 March 1936 which looks deeper and further. 'My German compatriots, there is very much which we have to make good before our own history and before our Lord God. Once His grace was upon us; and we were not worthy to keep it. Providence withdrew its protection from

us, and our people were put down, put down
deeper perhaps than any people before. In
this dire need we learned to pray once more.
We learned to respect one another: we believed again in the virtues of a people: we
tried again to be better. So there arose a
new community; and this people of to-day
can no more be compared with the people
that lies behind us. It has become better,
decenter, nobler. We feel it: the grace of the
Lord now turns again at the last towards us,
and in this hour we fall on our knees and
pray to the Almighty to bless us, and to
give us strength to endure the struggle for
the freedom and the future and the honour
and the peace of our people. So help us
God.'

II

Carlyle interpreted Cromwell as a hero. He
was interpreting him in terms of the German Romanticism with which he was im-
bued—a Romanticism inspired with the
idea of a pantheistic universe, which sees in

the people an incarnation of God, and in the hero or leader the incarnation of the people. A Cromwell so interpreted has his analogies with the modern leader, similarly exalted, and similarly idealized, by the permanent German spirit of Romanticism. The leader to-day can also appeal to the 'evidences' of Providence. He can also regard himself—or rather, will he, nill he, he can be regarded by others—as sent by a foreseeing Power. 'Among us Germans', the German Church Minister said, on the eve of the Christmas of 1936, 'a man has arisen who has given renewed direction and steadiness to our life, in that he has brought us once more into the Divine order.' That Divine order, the Minister went on to say, 'was the community ordained by God, and decided by blood... the people; and to serve it was to offer real service to God Himself....' This is Romantic heroism *in excelsis*. But has it, when it is analysed, any real bearing on the historic interpretation of Cromwell? Does it represent, in any respect, the mind of Cromwell and his contemporaries?

Cromwell himself, as has already been said, never thought of himself as a leader or hero. He was simply a constable, keeping the peace in his little parish. Nor was he regarded as a hero or leader by his contemporaries, even when they stood at his side and belonged to his following. There was a time when John Lilburn, the Leveller, spoke of him as 'the most absolute single-hearted great man in England'. But Lilburn turned, and accused him of high treason; and there was no jury in England which would ever convict honest John for the contumacy of his free speech. No sweeping enthusiasm ever surrounded Cromwell: the gusts of opinion beat steadily on him during his life, as gusts of wind shook the house in which he lay dying during his last stormy days. In the divided and tumultuous England in which he lived he was a great and elemental force; but he was surrounded by other forces, and he was never an engulfing vortex. He was not a sole and accredited leader; and he led no sole accredited party. Parties, in any sense in which they are known to us, were still unknown in his days. There were only trends of opinion, mainly religious, but partly (and consequentially) political. A dominant trend of Independent opinion, expressed in the army of which he was General, carried Cromwell along— sometimes struggling, and always seeking for a general healing and settling—on the current of its tide. But there were also other trends and other tides; and in the swirling eddies in which they met he felt himself battered and buffeted, sighing to 'have lived under his woodside...rather than undertook such a government', or attempted so arduous a work of steering.

If there was something heroic in this, it was the ordinary workaday heroism of doing a job; preventing men from 'running their heads one against another'; keeping things going; getting the business of the country done. It was something in the ordinary tradition of England, before his time and afterwards: the Duke of Wellington, if he had lived in Cromwell's day, would not have done very differently, nor would Cromwell, if he had lived in the days of Wellington, have done very differently from the Duke. The heroic interpretation of Cromwell must condescend to an ordinary level of heroism: if he was *fortis Agamemnon*, others had been brave before, and others were also to be brave afterwards. But there remains, in the general quality and temper of those times—not in him only, but in the general body of the Puritan cause —a bravery and a heroism which cannot but seem exceptional. Was the English people, for once at any rate in its history, transfigured? Did it become a people of one heart—an incarnation, in its own view, of the purpose of God; brought once more into the Divine order, with all its members serving God because they served the community ordained by God? If Cromwell himself was not a hero in the Romantic sense, was the people he governed a people, for the time being, in that sense?

Cromwell, as we have seen, had a doctrine of the two peoples. One was 'the people of England'; the other was 'the people of God' in England—'a people that are to God as the apple of His eye'. By the people of God he meant the Puritans; and the Puritans were, in his view, the leaven that could stir the English people to be what he called 'the best people in the world'. This doctrine and this view demand close consideration. Here, if anywhere, the analogy between Cromwellian England and the Germany of National Socialism exists; and if it does not exist here, it is not a true and essential analogy.

The core of Cromwell's doctrine of the nature of the people is a religious core. It is belief in God, through Jesus Christ, which makes the people of God; and it is the people of God who make a whole people good, because they make it serve the purposes of God. There is nothing physical in this conception. There is no belief in blood or race. Cromwell is thinking entirely in terms of the mind ('truly, these things do respect the souls of men, and the spirits, which are the men'); and thinking in those terms he can welcome into the core and central leaven of the people all who are of the right mind—'Scots, English, Jews, Gentiles, Presbyterians, Anabaptists, and all.' It is true that Cromwell and his Puritan contemporaries cherished a sort of nationalism; but the community or nation for which they cherished this feeling was a community decided not by blood but by faith. The English nation for which they were passionate was a nation by adoption and grace, after the manner of the Old Testament—'a new Israel, a chosen people, directly covenanted with God.'[24] This may be called a religious nationalism. It is a form of nationalism in which the nation is not a religion, or the object of a cult, but, on the very contrary, religion and cult are the nation, and *they* constitute the foundation of its being. It is therefore a nationalism which runs easily and naturally into internationalism. There is nothing exclusive in the conception of 'a people of God' forming the core and leaven of a whole nation. The chosen people of one nation, and the whole of that nation through them, have a community and a fellowship with the chosen peoples of other nations, and with other nations through them. Cromwell himself and the Puritans generally were good internationalists. He could tell his Parliament himself that 'all the interests of the Protestants...all the interests in Christendom, are the same as yours'. Religion might constitute a chosen people; but it also constituted an international community of chosen peoples. It is true that this international community was itself exclusive. Cromwell could not transcend, on the premises from which he started, the idea of an international community limited to the Protestant world. Nor could he transcend, on the same premises, the idea of a martial and militant internationalism, engaged in a natural and providential enmity with the Roman Catholic world gathered under the leadership of Spain. But if his internationalism was exclusive, and even militant, his nationalism had never an exclusive quality. It was based too much on religion to exclude from its generous pale any man or body of men who professed that sovereign cause.

His nationalism was the less pronounced because, such as it was, it was always combined with a stern and rigorous sense of the direct and immediate responsibility of each individual to God. Deeper than the internationalism of the Puritan lay his individualism. He might serve the chosen people, and through the chosen people he might serve the nation; but the service of which he always thought was the ultimate and lonely service which he owed directly to God. Community was not a word which bulked largely in his vocabulary; and he would never have said that service to the community was service to God Himself. Cromwell, essentially an Independent, and by the cast of his own mind an individual Seeker as well as an Independent, had no conception that even 'the people of God', though they might be of 'one heart and mutual love', were a uniform community, gathered in a single order or inspired by a corporate devotion. 'When I say the people of God, I mean the large comprehension of them *under the several forms of godliness* in this nation.'[25]

III

All periods of revolution have naturally a certain similarity. They all carry with them an exhilarating sense of entry into a new and regenerated life. They all involve a closing of the ranks around the ideal of the new life; and that involves in turn both internal and external consequences. Internally there will be an impatience with dissident and anti-revolutionary elements: the sense of *fraternité*, as it was called in 1789, or of *Volkstum* and *Volksgemeinschaft*, as it has been called since 1933, will be deeply felt; and in the strength of that sense there will be an insistence on unity, even at the cost of repression—on the republic one and indivisible; on the *Reich*, and on the *Volk* behind the *Reich*, which is one and undivided in blood and policy. Externally the glow of a new life and the sense of a new solidarity will exert an expansive force: the revolution will become militant: it will seek to assert itself in the world, and to vindicate its worth on the public stage of the nations.

The Puritan Revolution shares with the German Revolution of to-day (as it also shares with the French Revolution of 1789) these common characteristics. It also shares, or seems to share, another characteristic— the figure of the revolutionary leader, a basalt figure emerging among the fires and in the eruption, a column and a symbol of the movement of mind from which he has come. But though these are common characteristics of revolutions, each revolution is essentially unique. It has its own spiritual foundations: they are its own peculiar property; and they vest it in turn with a property, or quality, which is particularly and peculiarly its own. The spiritual foundations of the revolution of Cromwell's day were religious.[26] They were hewn from the common rock of European Protestantism, even if they were quarried in a particular English quarry. They were hewn in the seventeenth century; and they have the particular quality of an age in which the religious motive was still the dominant motive. The

spiritual foundations of the National Socialist Revolution are different. They are hewn
from the particular tradition of Germany.
They go back to the Romantic exaltation of
the *Volk* which became current at the end
of the eighteenth century: they go back,
behind that, to the *Urvolk* of the German
woods. So far as religion is part of their
foundations, it is a religion not of theism
(in any form, Protestant or Catholic), but of
pantheism—a religion of a universally im-
manent God, who, instead of being found
and worshipped by 'a people of God',
finds himself, and incarnates himself, in
a whole people, which in turn incarnates
itself in the leader of the people. The God
who becomes a people, and the people
which becomes identified with its leader, are
not the God and the people which presented
themselves to the mind of Cromwell. They
are not the God and the people who present
themselves to the minds of most modern
Englishmen. The community 'ordained by

God and decided by blood' does not belong
to our way of thinking. It belongs to
tribalism—even if tribalism wears the
mantle of a pantheistic philosophy.

All revolutions exaggerate. At any rate
there are always revolutionary sections
which exaggerate the tenets of revolution.
It may be that the theory of tribalism goes
far beyond the ideas of the leader of the
German people, and far beyond the con-
victions of the great bulk of its members.
There are utterances of the National Socialist party, and above all of its leader, which
breathe the same spirit of religious conviction, and show something of the same instinct for religious liberty, which inspired
the speeches of Cromwell. One of the
'points' of the original party programme,
of February 1920, proclaims: 'We demand
the liberty of all religious confessions in
the State, so far as they do not imperil its
stability, or offend against the sentiments of
the German race in matters of social ethics

and private morality.' Here there is an ideal of religious liberty—qualified, it is true; but then it was also qualified in the ideas and practice of Cromwell. When the party eventually came into power, its leader, speaking as Chancellor, on 23 March 1933, went even further. 'The national government', he said, 'sees in the two Christian confessions the most important factors for the maintenance of our people's life.... The fight against a materialist conception of life, and for the restoration of a real community of the people, serves the interests of the German nation equally with those of the Christian faith.' Here, in the spirit of Cromwell, and almost in his words, the leader of National Socialism connects 'the Interest of Christians' with 'the Interest of the Nation'. But a little later, in a speech of 30 January 1934, he has already parted from Cromwell. The one thing which Cromwell firmly believed was that political uniformity did not require, or involve, religious uniformity. On that belief, like the rest of the Independents, he took his stand equally against Anglicans and Presbyterians. The leader of National Socialism, on the contrary, urges that a new system of political uniformity requires and involves, from the Protestant Churches of Germany (still organized in separate territorial bodies, which reflect the disintegration of the past), a corresponding new system of religious uniformity. 'We all live in the expectation that the union of the Evangelical territorial churches and confessions in a German *Reichskirche* will give a real satisfaction to the longing of those who believe that they are bound to fear, in the disintegration of Evangelical life, a weakening of the strength of Evangelical faith. Since the National Socialist State has this year shown its respect for the strength of the Christian confessions, it expects the confessions to show the same respect for the strength of the National Socialist State.'

Here the proviso originally attached to religious liberty—that it should not imperil the stability of the State—shows its cutting edge. To Cromwell 'the Interest of the Nation' was subordinate to 'the Interest of Christians'. To the leader of National Socialism 'the Interest of the Nation' has become dominant.

But these comparisons only lead us down a blind alley. We come out again at the same door at which we went in. Our parallels show us mainly difference, with occasional glimpses of likeness; and to compare two things which are partly alike, but differ even more than they agree, may make even more for bewilderment than it does for enlightenment. But it is one of the habits of men in revolutionary times, when they have broken loose from their moorings, to comfort themselves by thinking that they are only engaged in the restoration of their own past, or that they have a precedent and an example in the past of some other country.

It has been said that 'restoration is always also revolution'; it may also be said that revolution is often also restoration—and sometimes imitation.[27] The German revolution of our days proceeds on the idea of the restoration of the German past: it also proceeds—or some of its thinkers proceed —on the assumption of analogy and precedent in the English past. It is true that there is a sense in which Germany (and, we may also add, Italy) is going through a stage of development through which we went some centuries ago. It is the stage of unification; of the acquisition of national homogeneity; of the attainment of a sure and tranquil basis of national life, on which men are agreed, and in the strength of which they can quietly pass on their ways upon their lawful occasions. One of the observations which every visitor to England naturally and inevitably makes is the observation of the fact of national homogeneity and a generally agreed basis of national life.[28] Such homogeneity, and such an agreed basis, have to be won, and have been won, by an effort.

'Tantae molis erat Romanam condere gentem.'

But it was not in the days of Cromwell that homogeneity and an agreed basis were first, or finally, won in England. If any man 'imposed the yoke of peace' in England, it was Henry VIII rather than Cromwell; and it is Henry VIII rather than Cromwell who is the precedent and example for the totalitarian leader. If any Revolution ended by assuring to England an agreed basis of national life, it was the Whig Revolution of 1688, rather than the Puritan Revolution of the previous generation; and it is the Whig Revolution (with its prosaic sobriety, its compromises and its common sense), rather than the Puritan Revolution, which is the natural analogy and precedent for those who desire to achieve a permanent political settlement.

Cromwell had indeed a genuine passion for healing and settling; for unification: for an England settled within on the rock of religious liberty and reformation of manners, and great and glorious without because she was great and glorious within. But it was not given to him, or to those who thought with him, to achieve these things. Theirs was the triumphant but temporary explosion of a minority; and it passed. They left indeed a permanent legacy to England —the legacy of an ineradicable Nonconformity: the legacy of the Free Churches: the legacy of a permanent idea of liberty, political as well as religious and civil, but pre-eminently and particularly the latter. But because they used force in the service of liberty (disbelieving in the force by which they acted, and yet acting by force in spite of their disbelief), they also left another legacy—the legacy of hatred of a standing army; the legacy of a rooted dislike of compulsory godliness; the legacy of contempt for the paradox of their cause, which could be, and was, interpreted as cant and hypocrisy. Yet their work was not unaccomplished. When they turned, as they did after 1660, from a victorious minority into a minority struggling for the just rights of minorities (toleration; liberty of worship; equality of access to education and civic rights), they came into their own, and they gave to England a great gift, essential and indispensable to her genuine tradition—the gift of the still small voice (after wind and earthquake and fire) of human liberty. The defeated Cromwells of hundreds of town and village chapels, scattered over England, carried on the heart of the cause of the victorious Cromwell, purged and purified; and the dust that lay in his unknown and unregarded grave still lived. So his actings fulfilled the good pleasure of God, and served their generations; and his rest was durable.

NOTES

1 The pit was beneath the gallows at Tyburn, near Marble Arch. 'Where Connaught Square now stands, a yard or two beneath the street,...lies the dust of the great Protector.' C. H. Firth, *Life of Cromwell*, p. 452.

2 Nobody who has lived in Cambridge can have failed to feel the peculiar genius of the Eastern Counties, with their far and pensive distances. In an agricultural age they must have been well populated, by a sober class of tolerably prosperous farmers, who were akin to the soil and the far-spread open sky. Here, in the sixteenth century, the Reformation struck its roots; and 'the fenland seminary' of Cambridge, drawing on the country round, became its particular home. In the seventeenth century it was the district round Cambridge which largely peopled New England; and it was the same district which was the peculiar home of Independency, and the recruiting ground of the Ironsides. Oliver Cromwell and Isaac Newton both represent, in their different ways, its deep sense of the fundamental rules which govern nature and human life: they both served, in their different capacities, in

'The army of unalterable law'.

Even to-day the Congregationalists and Baptists are stronger in Huntingdon and Cambridge than in any other district of England. (Frank Tillyard, article in the *Sociological Review* on 'The Distribution of the Free Churches in England', January 1935.)

3 George Unwin, *Studies in Economic History*, p. 341 (controverting Seeley's thesis in *The Expansion of England*). On Unwin's general view of Society and its relation to the State, see p. 459. He remarks, in another passage (p. 28), that 'it is worthy of remark that, whilst the main feature of British history since the seventeenth century has been the remoulding of the State by a powerful Society, the main feature of German history in the same period has been the remoulding of Society by a powerful State'.

4 Carl Schmitt, *Der Begriff des Politischen*, pp. 54–5. The author argues that political thought and instinct show themselves in the capacity of distinguishing friend and foe: the zenith of *die grosze Politik* is the moment in which the foe is recognized, concretely and clearly, as foe. Cromwell's speech of 1656 against Spain is cited as a particular evidence of this doctrine: 'Für die Neuzeit sehe ich den mächstigsten Ausbruch einer solchen Feindschaft—stärker als das gewisz nicht zu unterschätzende *écrasez l'infâme* des 18. Jahrhunderts, stärker als der Franzosenhasz des Freiherrn von Stein, stärker sogar als Lenins vernichtende Sätze gegen den Bourgeois und den Westlichen

Kapitalismus—in Cromwells Kampf gegen das papistische Spanien.' Dr Schmitt proceeds to quote some sentences from the speech—sentences striking enough, in their isolation; but, in their general context, entirely removed from any idea of *die grosze Politik*.

5 Quoted from the *Clarke Papers*, vol. III, p. 207, in G. M. Trevelyan's *England under the Stuarts*, pp. 322–3.

6 *England under the Stuarts*, p. 322.

7 The Liberal Party, the party of Free Trade, was also the party of Nonconformity in its hey-day; and 'the Nonconformist Conscience' (a term of derision, like the term 'Puritan' in its original usage, but a term of derision which turns to praise) attached a peculiar consecration to the doctrine of Free Trade. The Labour Party, which may be termed the party of Free Labour (devoted to the rights and the liberties of the trade unions), has drawn many of its leaders from the circles of the Free Churches; and the cause of the free church-man and that of the free 'tradesman' (in the sense in which the term is still used colloquially in Northern England) have obvious analogies and sympathies.

8 During the battle of Dunbar, on the morning of 3 September 1650, 'the Lord-General made a halt, and sang the Hundred-and-seventeenth Psalm'. But he only halted till the horse could gather for the pursuit; and the Hundred-and-seventeenth Psalm is a psalm of two verses only.

9 It is curious to reflect that the space of five and a half years was also the space given to Julius Caesar. Mommsen, in a famous passage of his *History of Rome* (vol. IV, p. 557, in the English translation), remarks: 'Caesar ruled as King of Rome for five years and a half, not half as long as Alexander; in the intervals of seven great campaigns, which allowed him to stay not more than fifteen months altogether in the capital of his empire, he regulated the destinies of the world for the present and the future.... Thus he worked and created, as never any mortal did before or after him; and as a worker and creator he still, after wellnigh two thousand years, lives in the memory of the nations.' Cromwell's five years and a half were more pedestrian; and they were years uninterrupted by campaigns. But it would be curious to compare the fundamental significance of the five and a half years from 49 to 44 B.C. with that of the five and a half years from A.D. 1653 to 1658. Perhaps the balance would not tilt all on one side.

10 The passage deserves quotation in full. 'The mind is the man. If that be kept pure, a man signifies somewhat; if not, I would very fain see what difference there is betwixt him and a beast. He hath only some activity to do some more mischief.' (Speech of 17 September 1656.) This is like Goethe:

'Er nennt's Vernunft, und braucht's allein
Nur tierischer als jedes Tier zu sein.'

11 Quoted in C. H. Firth, *Life of Cromwell*, p. 205. The mention of the Jews deserves notice. Cromwell was personally favourable to the cause of the Jews, when they petitioned, in 1655, for freedom to reside for purposes of trade and to practise their religion. 'The fierce multitude of the Jews' had been ordered to leave England by Edward I in 1290; and there had been no Jews in England, except by stealth, for three and a half centuries. In the time of the Commonwealth the Jews were beginning to settle again in London; the petition of 1655 was a petition for the legal recognition of such settlement. The petition was referred to a committee of the Council; the committee co-opted two judges; the two judges gave it as their opinion that there was no law forbidding the settlement of Jews. Nothing was done by the committee; but the opinion of the judges opened the way for the quiet and unmolested return of the Jews to England. (S. R. Gardiner, *History of the Commonwealth and Protectorate*, vol. II, p. 101; vol. IV, pp. 11–15.)

12 C. H. Firth, *Life of Cromwell*, p. 369.

13 *Ibidem*, p. 483.

14 The contemporary is Baxter, quoted in C. H. Firth's *Life of Cromwell*, p. 148. The man who noted Cromwell's gift for saying little, but making others talk, was Sir William Waller, quoted in Firth, *ibidem*, p. 119.

15 M. R. James, *The Apocryphal New Testament*, pp. 25–6.

16 A. D. Lindsay, *Essentials of Democracy*, pp. 19, 36. Cromwell's stipulation of 1647, that 'the spirits and temper of the nation must be prepared to receive and go along with' any plan for the future of England, recurs again in his argument to the army in the midsummer of 1648. The Agitators of the regiments were pressing for a hammer-stroke of force. Cromwell pleaded for co-operation with the friendly elements in Parliament and an agreed solution. 'What we and they gain in a free way is better than twice so much in a forced way, and will be more truly ours and our posterity's....That you have by force I look upon as nothing. I do not know that force is to be used except we cannot get what is for the good of the kingdom without it.' (Quoted in Firth, *Life of Cromwell*, p. 169.)

17 Wilhelm Dibelius, *England* (English translation), p. 495. 'Democratic forms', he adds, 'are merely so much stage scenery, behind which the few, or, it may be, a single individual, exercise almost unlimited command.' But Dibelius also remarks, a few pages later (p. 504), that 'the English achievement is, in the last analysis, not the individual achievement of single statesmen...but the collective achievement of the Anglo-Saxon race. England can live without great men... longer than any other country.' National traits have a way of inverting themselves suddenly, according to the demands of the context.

18 'No theory of the divine right of an able man to govern the incapable multitude blinded his

eyes to the fact that self-government was the inheritance and the right of Englishmen.' Firth, *Life of Cromwell*, p. 483.

19 This passage merits a fuller quotation. 'I can say in the presence of God, in comparison of whom we are but poor creeping ants upon the earth, I would have lived under my woodside....' Quoted in Firth, *Life of Cromwell*, p. 440.

20 The poet was Landor. Forster quoted his verdict as 'indisputably true' as late as 1839, in his *Statesmen of the Commonwealth* (Firth, *Life of Cromwell*, p. 476); and Forster was a Liberal in politics.

21 These passages are drawn from various periods of Cromwell's life. The first belongs to the period of the political debates in the New Model Army in 1647 (Firth, *Life of Cromwell*, p. 180). The second comes from a letter to Colonel Hammond, in whose hands Charles I then lay at Carisbrooke Castle, at the end of November 1648 (*ibidem*, p. 213). The third comes from his speech to Parliament in July 1653 (*ibidem*, p. 331). The last comes from a letter addressed from Ireland to the Speaker of the Parliament, in November 1649 (quoted in G. M. Trevelyan, *England under the Stuarts*, p. 327).

22 This conception of the two peoples is admirably explained in Firth, *Life of Cromwell*, pp. 482–3.

23 These unforgettable words (quoted in Firth, *ibidem*, p. 253) show clearly how Cromwell could make the English language become a trumpet.

103

There is music too, if less magnificent, in an earlier passage that goes back to 1643: 'I had rather have a plain russet-coated captain that knows what he fights for and loves what he knows, than that which you call a gentleman, and is nothing else' (*ibidem*, p. 92).

24 These words were used by the writer in an essay on 'The Reformation and Nationality' which appeared in the *Modern Churchman* in 1932 (pp. 329–43). In that essay (written before the triumph of National Socialism in Germany, and with no thought of the tenets of National Socialism) it was argued that there was an element of 'induced nationality' in the Reformation, derived from the study and imitation of the life of the Jewish nation, as recorded in the Old Testament. 'The example of the Jewish nation is a recurrent theme in the literature of the Reformation, and the Hebraism of the sixteenth century may almost be counted as a form of nationality—a form which reappeared in our English Commonwealth of the next century. Each of the Reformed peoples is encouraged to regard itself as a new Israel, a chosen people, directly covenanted with God.'

25 Quoted in Firth, *Life of Cromwell*, pp. 482–3.

26 I. Deane Jones, in his book on *The English Revolution, 1603–1714*, has remarked that 'most wars begin as a crusade, but all end as a business.' (Perhaps he had in mind the war of 1914–18.) The present writer, in an introduction to the book, was led to suggest that our Civil War, unlike most

wars, began as a business, but ended as a crusade. It began in disputes about national finance and the proper methods of meeting a deficit; but the religious issue, always present in the depths of men's minds, soon rose to the top, and became the dominant issue. Charles I died as a convinced martyr to the cause of Anglicanism: Cromwell lived and acted, in all his public days, as a convinced professor of Independency.

27 The dictum is that of Mommsen, speaking (if the writer's memory is correct) of Sulla's restoration of the powers of the Roman senate and aristocracy.... The tendency of revolutions to profess the character of restorations has often been illustrated in history. The Reformation was a restoration of *prisca fides*: the French Revolution was a return to the original rights of man 'when he came from the hand of his Maker': the English Revolution which began in 1640 was a return to 'the good old decrepit law of Magna Charta'. The revolutionary who is anxious for precedent and parallel may sometimes arm himself by reprinting revolutionary literature of the past, whether native or foreign. Ulrich von Hutten went back to the anti-papal literature of the medieval War of Investitures: Henry VIII had the *Defensor Pacis* of Marsilius of Padua exhumed and translated; and in 1648 an English Member of Parliament caused a translation of the Huguenot *Vindiciae contra Tyrannos* (which had appeared in 1579) to be prepared and printed in London. Sometimes the exhuming

of past history, from a previous revolutionary epoch, equally serves the turn of the revolutionary. The Whigs before 1689 went back to the reign of Richard II. William Godwin the radical (the author of *Political Justice*) published a *History of the Commonwealth*—the first book I remember reading on that period—in the years 1824–28. We are none of us without respect for the past—not even the most radical of us—especially when it can be pressed into the service of the present.

28 The observation has been brilliantly and sympathetically made by Dr Adolf Löwe in a pamphlet recently published by the Hogarth Press, entitled *The Price of Liberty*.

Lightning Source UK Ltd.
Milton Keynes UK
UKHW010636190122
397374UK00001B/39

9 781107 660717